MW01471211

Georgia, My State Biographies

Tomochichi

by Doraine Bennett

STATE STANDARDS PUBLISHING

Your State • Your Standards • Your Grade Level

Dear Educators, Librarians and Parents . . .

Thank you for choosing the *"Georgia, My State" Biographies* series! We have designed this series to support the Georgia Department of Education's Georgia Performance Standards for second grade social studies. Each book in the series has been written at appropriate grade level as measured by the ATOS Readability Formula for Books (Accelerated Reader), the Lexile Framework for Reading, and the Fountas & Pinnell Benchmark Assessment System for Guided Reading, and has been evaluated by a reading program consultant to ensure grade-level appropriateness. Photographs and/or illustrations, captions, time line and other design elements have been included to provide supportive visual messaging to enhance text comprehension. Glossary and Word Index sections introduce key new words and help young readers develop skills in locating and combining information. A reproducible Teacher's Guide, available separately, provides opportunities for expanded supervised learning experiences. We wish you all success in using the *"Georgia, My State" Biographies* series to meet your student or child's learning needs. For additional sources of information, see www.georgiaencyclopedia.org.

Jill Ward, President

Publisher
State Standards Publishing, LLC
5157 Hwy. 219, Suite 5
Fortson, GA 31808
USA
1.866.740.3056
www.statestandardspublishing.com

Library of Congress Cataloging-in-Publication Data
Bennett, Doraine, 1953-
  Tomochichi / by Doraine Bennett.
      p. cm. -- (Georgia, my state biographies)
  Includes index.
  ISBN-13: 978-1-935077-06-0 (hardcover)
  ISBN-10: 1-935077-06-6 (hardcover)
  ISBN-13: 978-1-935077-13-8 (pbk.)
  ISBN-10: 1-935077-13-9 (pbk.)
  1. Tomo-chi-chi, d. 1739--Juvenile literature. 2. Yamassee Indians--Biography--Juvenile literature. 3. Yamassee Indians--History--Juvenile literature. 4. Georgia--History--Colonial period, ca. 1600-1775--Juvenile literature. 5. Oglethorpe, James Edward, 1696-1785--Juvenile literature. I. Title.
  E99.Y22T653 2008
  970.004'97--dc22
    [B]   2008028943

Copyright © 2008 by State Standards Publishing, LLC. All rights reserved. No part of this book may be reproduced, stored, or transmitted in any form or by any means without prior written permission from the publisher.

Published in the United States of America.

Table of Contents

Tomochichi 5

The Georgia Colony 7

An Exciting Trip 17

Georgia's Friend 21

Glossary 22

Word Index 23

Tomochichi was chief of the Yamacraw Indian tribe.

TimeLine

1728
Builds town on Savannah River

Tomochichi

Tomochichi was born in 1640. He was the chief of the **Yamacraw** Indian tribe. He was tall and strong. He was a brave warrior and a wise leader. Tomochichi built a Yamacraw town on the **Savannah River**.

People came from England to start Georgia.

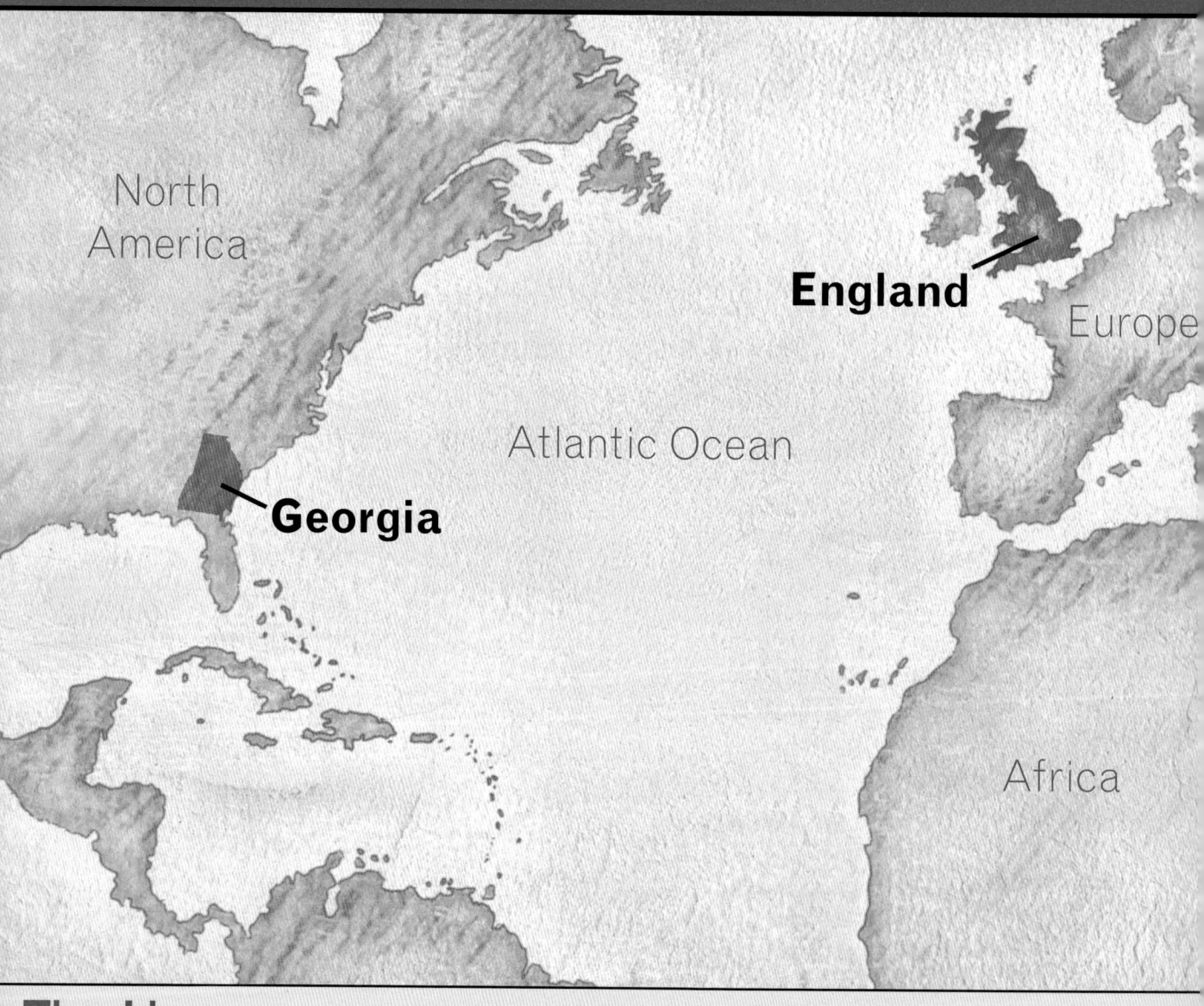

North America

England

Europe

Atlantic Ocean

Georgia

Africa

TimeLine

1728
Builds town on Savannah River

1733
Meets James Oglethorpe

6

The Georgia Colony

Tomochichi **traded** with John and Mary Musgrove. They traded skins, tools, and other things the Indians needed. One day, Mary brought James Oglethorpe to meet Tomochichi. James wanted to start the **colony** of Georgia. He wanted to make homes in a new land.

The people from England needed land to live on.

TimeLine

1728
Builds town on Savannah River

1733
Meets James Oglethorpe

James brought people from **England** with him to Georgia. They needed land to build their new homes. They did not know the Indian language. They could not ask Tomochichi for land to live on.

Tomochichi gave land to build Savannah.

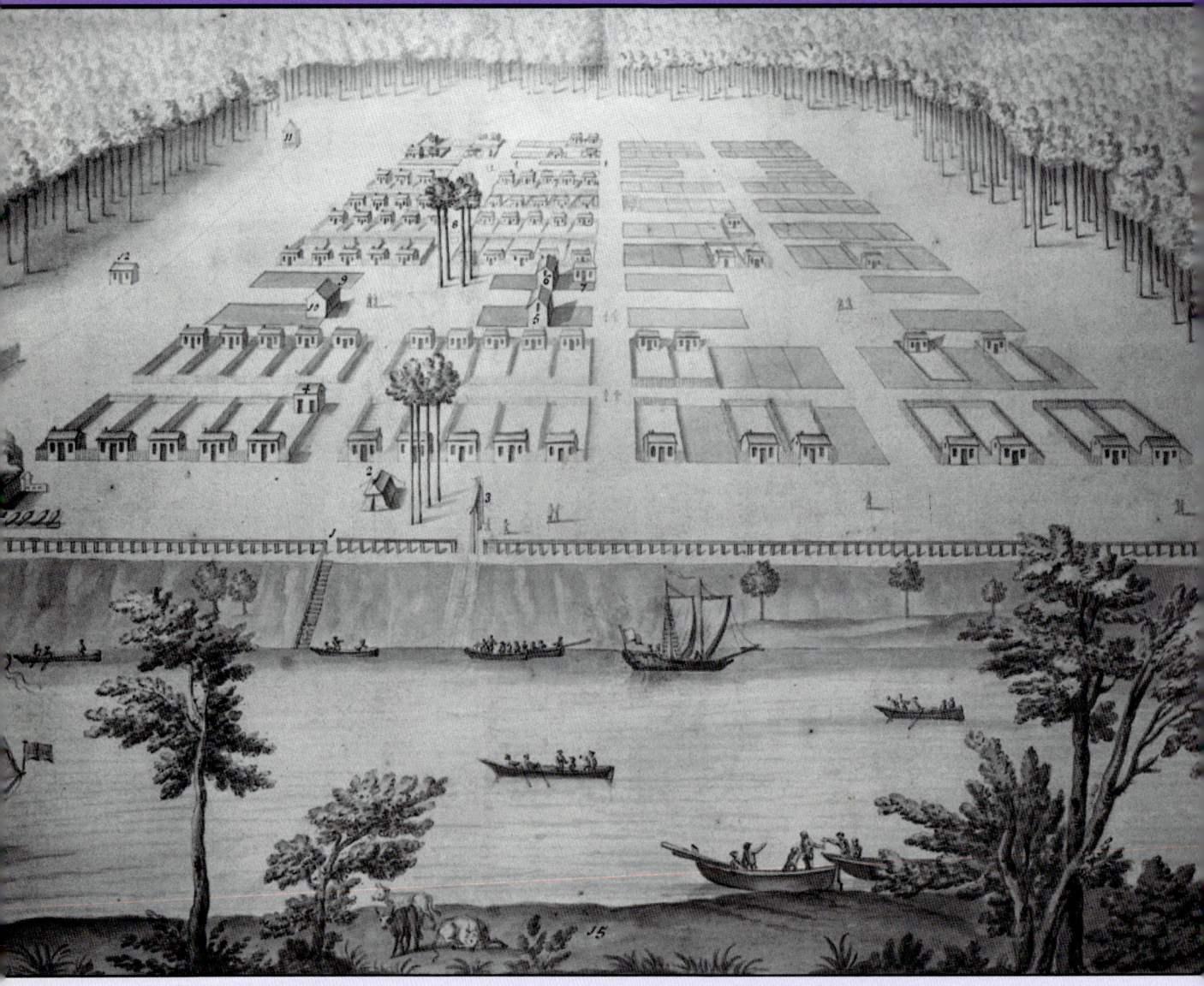

TimeLine

1728
Builds town on Savannah River

1733
Meets James Oglethorpe

Mary spoke English. She also spoke the Indian language. Mary helped James talk to Tomochichi. Tomochichi gave land to build the city of **Savannah**. It was the first city in Georgia.

James Oglethorpe taught Tomochichi and his nephew.

TimeLine

1728
Builds town on Savannah River

1733
Meets James Oglethorpe

Tomochichi liked the English people. He helped them learn to grow **crops** in the hot weather. They grew crops like corn, rice, and the **indigo** plant. Tomochichi asked James to teach his nephew to read and write English.

Tomochichi helped James make friends.

TimeLine

1728
Builds town on Savannah River

1733
Meets James Oglethorpe

Tomochichi helped James meet the other **Native Americans**. James became friends with the chiefs of the Indian tribes. James asked the English to be kind to Tomochichi and the other Native Americans.

Tomochichi met many important people in England.

TimeLine

1728
Builds town on Savannah River

1733
Meets James Oglethorpe

An Exciting Trip

James asked Tomochichi to sail to England with him. They went on James's boat. Tomochichi took his wife and nephew. They met King George the Second and Queen Caroline. Georgia was named after the king.

1734
Goes to England

Tomochichi told about his trip to England.

TimeLine

1728
Builds town on Savannah River

1733
Meets James Oglethorpe

18

Tomochichi told the people in England stories about Georgia. The people liked him and his family. Tomochichi came home. He told the people what he saw in England.

1734
Goes to England

The people made a monument to thank Tomochichi.

TimeLine

1728
Builds town on Savannah River

1733
Meets James Oglethorpe

Georgia's Friend

Tomochichi lived to be almost a hundred years old. He was a good friend to James and the people of Georgia. The people of Georgia put a large rock **monument** in Savannah. It helps us remember Georgia's friend, Tomochichi.

1734
Goes to England

1739
Dies

Glossary

crops – plants or animals that are grown to eat, to trade, or to sell for money.

colony – a group of people making homes in a new land. A colony belongs to the country that started it.

England – The country that started Georgia.

indigo – a plant used to make blue dye.

monument – a statue or thing to help people remember a friend or an important person.

Native Americans – Indian tribes who lived in America before people from other countries arrived.

Savannah – the first city started in Georgia. It is located on the Savannah River.

Savannah River – the river that runs through the city of Savannah.

traded – buying and selling things, or giving things to a trader in exchange for something else.

Yamacraw – a group of Native Americans who lived in Georgia. Yamacraws were part of the Creek Indian tribe.

Word Index

born — 5

chief — 5, 15

colony — 7

crops — 13

England — 9, 17, 19

friend — 7, 15, 21

Georgia — 7, 9, 11, 17, 19, 21

indigo — 13

James Oglethorpe — 7, 9, 11, 13, 15, 17, 21

King George the Second — 17

land — 9, 11

Mary Musgrove — 7, 11

monument — 20

Native Americans — 15

Savannah — 5, 11, 21

Savannah River — 5

traded — 7

warrior — 5

Yamacraw — 5

Image Credits

Cover	Courtesy of Hargrett Rare Book & Manuscript Library, University of Georgia Libraries
p. 4	Courtesy of Hargrett Rare Book & Manuscript Library, University of Georgia Libraries
p. 6	Copyright © Stephen Sweet, fotolia.com
p. 8	Picture Collection, The Branch Libraries, The New York Public Library, Astor, Lenox and Tilden Foundations
p. 10	Courtesy of Hargrett Rare Book & Manuscript Library, University of Georgia Libraries
p. 12	Courtesy of Hargrett Rare Book & Manuscript Library, University of Georgia Libraries
p. 14	Picture Collection, The Branch Libraries, The New York Public Library, Astor, Lenox and Tilden Foundations
p. 16	Picture Collection, The Branch Libraries, The New York Public Library, Astor, Lenox and Tilden Foundations
p. 18	Courtesy of V & J Duncan Antique Maps, Prints and Books: Savannah, Georgia
p. 20	Courtesy of Edwin Jackson, Carl Vinson Institute of Government, University of Georgia

About the Author

Doraine Bennett has a degree in professional writing from Columbus State University in Columbus, Georgia and has been writing and teaching writing for over twenty years. She has authored numerous articles in magazines for both children and adults and is the editor of the National Infantry Association's *Infantry Bugler* magazine. Doraine enjoys reading and writing books and articles for children. She lives in Georgia with her husband, Cliff.